D0622093

The Blood
That Keeps Singing

La sangre
que sigue cantando

selected poems of
Clemente Soto Vélez

translated by/traducción de:
Martín Espada and Camilo Pérez-Bustillo

CURBSTONE PRESS

Muchas gracias to Cola Franzen, Leo Cabranes-Grant, and Roberto Márquez, who critiqued the English translation of the poems; to Rebeca Mingura and Elizabeth McGlynn, who assembled and computerized the manuscript; to Katherine Gilbert-Espada, María de la Luz Bautista-Pérez and Centli Pérez-Bautista, for being there; and to all the others who have supported us in carrying out this work.

This book is dedicated to Amanda Soto Vélez

Front cover photograph by Rafael (Changui) Díaz
Cover design by Stone Graphics
Printed in the U.S.

Some of these poems have appeared in the following publications:
Agni Review (#29/30), Boston University, Boston, MA: #18 from *La tierra prometida* (*The Promised Land*); #3 from *Caballo de palo* (*The Wooden Horse*). Translations only.
Hanging Loose (#52), Brooklyn, NY: #29 from *La tierra prometida* (*The Promised Land*). Original and translation.
Minnesota Review (#33), State University of New York at Stony Brook, NY: #35 from *La tierra prometida* (*The Promised Land*). Translation only.
The foreword is a revised and expanded version of an essay which originally appeared in the *Minnesota Review*, #33.

This publication was supported in part by donations, and by a grant from The Connecticut Commission on the Arts, a state agency whose funds are recommended by the Governor and appropriated by the State Legislature.

ISBN: 0-915306-78-6   Library of Congress number: 91-55409

distributed by
InBook
Box 120470
East Haven, CT 06512

published by
CURBSTONE PRESS
321 Jackson Street
Willimantic, CT 06226

Contents/índice

FOREWORD

The poet Clemente Soto Vélez was born in January of 1905 in Lares, Puerto Rico. Even his birthplace is noteworthy: Lares, in 1868, was the site of Puerto Rico's most important uprising against Spain, known as the "Grito de Lares," an event still commemorated every September 23rd. Soto Vélez, born in Lares during the lifetime of many who had a first-hand memory of the brief, but significant insurrection, thus provides a link with more than a century of Puerto Rican resistance to first Spanish and then U.S. colonial rule, a resistance he came to personify.

In 1928, Soto Vélez co-founded a literary movement: La Atalaya de los Dioses (The Watchtower of the Gods). As defined by Josefina Rivera de Alvarez in *Literatura puertorriqueña: su proceso en el tiempo* (Madrid, 1983), this was a movement parallel to and influenced by European surrealism: innovative, experimental, devoted to a fragmentation and reconstruction of reality and language. Atalayismo quickly evolved into a major literary force in Puerto Rico. Aside from its avant-garde elements, however, Atalayismo also featured a strong political sensibility. The rise of Atalayismo coincided with the rise of the militant Nationalist Party, a mass movement for independence as powerful as any in Puerto Rican history. Its brilliant, charismatic leader, Harvard Law School graduate Pedro Albizu Campos, inspired the Atalayistas, and achieved the fusion of the island's political and literary vanguards. What emerged, as later described by Soto Vélez, was a "compact for unified struggle;" the leading poets of Puerto Rico committed themselves to "making revolution from the podiums." Soto Vélez and fellow poet Juan Antonio Corretjer, with whom he would form a lifelong friendship, became part of the governing body for the Nationalist Party.

Soto Vélez also became the editor of the Nationalist Party weekly newspaper, known as "Armas (Weapons)," whose masthead bore the following admonition: "Puerto Rican, the independence of Puerto Rico depends on the number of bullets in your belt," a slogan echoed at countless rallies across the island. He was an equally effective organizer, participating in the 1932 takeover of the Capitol building in San Juan, directing a clandestine cell in Caguas, and coordinating the Party Congress of 1935, also in Caguas. The first of several imprisonments took place during this time, in Guayama, as part of a crackdown on a strike of sugar cane workers led by Albizu Campos in 1934.

By 1936, Puerto Rico was nearing open revolution. Federal and island authorities engineered the repression of the Nationalist Party by indicting its leadership on charges of seditious conspiracy. Albizu Campos, Soto Vélez, Corretjer and five others were convicted after two trials, the second of which featured a jury handpicked by the governor of the island — appointed by President Roosevelt — the notorious General Blanton Winship. The "evidence" introduced against Soto Vélez included the statement on the masthead of "Armas."

Soto Vélez and Corretjer were chained together during their voyage into forced exile. Soto Vélez served his sentence from 1936 to 1942 in various prisons — at La Princesa in Puerto Rico while awaiting trial, and thereafter in federal penitentiaries at Atlanta, Georgia and Lewisburg, Pennsylvania — developing serious health problems which would plague him for life. His first published book, *Escalio* (Fallow Land), a collection of philosophical writings and one culminating poem, appeared while he was still incarcerated. While in Atlanta, he and Corretjer met fellow inmate Earl Browder, then General Secretary of the Communist Party, U.S.A., and participated in a study group which resulted in their leaving prison as dedicated Marxists. Soto Velez became a member of the Party in 1943.

Soto Vélez was paroled in 1940, upon the condition that he not return to Puerto Rico until the completion of his full sentence. Nevertheless, he returned to the island and was quickly re-arrested after delivering four fiery speeches within a few days of his release. He then served another two years of his sentence at the prison in Lewisburg. Following his ultimate release in 1942, Soto Vélez settled in New York City. He became an organizer for the American Labor Party, as well as the successful campaign manager for U.S. Congressional Representative Vito Marcantonio, one of his attorneys for the 1936 trials and subsequent appeals. During this time, Soto Vélez also founded the Puerto Rican Merchants' Association, a powerful organization of small shopkeepers.

Together with Corretjer, Consuelo Lee Tapia (Corretjer's wife), and another major poet, Julia de Burgos, Soto Vélez edited and wrote for an important political and literary weekly, *"Pueblos Hispanos,"* from 1943 to 1944. He also wrote for the journal *"Liberación"* from 1946 to 1949, a publication described by Juan Flores as "the main New York forum for progressive writers" in the

8

Spanish language at that time. He served as the editor of *"La Voz de Puerto Rico"* as well. Above all, Soto Vélez became, according to Efraín Barradas and other scholars, the founder of New York's contemporary Puerto Rican literary community, sponsoring and inspiring numerous writers over the years, deeply involved with such cultural organizations as the Ateneo Puertorriqueño de Nueva York and the Círculo de Escritores y Poetas Iberoamericanos. He has been honored for this dual role as writer and mentor many times: at the Festival Latino in New York, at a major symposium on his life and work at Seton Hall University, by the principal universities of Puerto Rico and the Dominican Republic, by the Instituto de Cultura Puertorriqueña and by PEN.

Soto Vélez was most prolific as a poet in the 1950s. He published *Abrazo interno (Internal Embrace)* in 1954, *Arboles (Trees)* in 1955, and *Caballo de palo (The Wooden Horse)*, a book which firmly established his literary reputation, in 1959. A monumental work, *La tierra prometida (The Promised Land)*, was published by the Instituto de Cultura Puertorriqueña in 1979. The Instituto also published his *Obra poetica*, the collected writings from his previous five books, in 1989. His current manuscript, as yet unpublished, is called *Mujer u ombre, ombre o mujer (Woman or Man, Man or Woman)*. His verses have been musicalized by the popular New Song artist, Roy Brown, and thus introduced to a new generation of Puerto Ricans.

Aesthetically, as well as politically, Soto Vélez is often reminiscent of the great Peruvian poet César Vallejo, especially in terms of Vallejo's *Poemas Humanos (Human Poems)* and *España, aparta de mí este cáliz (Spain, Take This Cup From Me)*, his poems about the Spanish Civil War. Roberto Márquez notes the similarity in "verbal and conceptual construction" between the two poets, in the use of personification, for example; note the masterful use of this device by Soto Vélez in "Those Trees," as they "wash/the abandoned house of affection/with their hearts." Márquez observes another close resemblance, aesthetically if not politically, with Chilean poet Vicente Huidobro, finding the same surrealistic "play on inversions" in works such as *Altazor*.

The poems of Soto Vélez are revolutionary in form: a cascade of surreal images, thriving on duality and contradiction, characterized by a forceful use of rhythm, repetition and alliteration. His later works are without punctuation, challenging traditional grammar and spelling, flavored with invented words; Soto Vélez actually created his own phonetic Spanish alphabet so that, he insists, no one could ever misspell a word. Though the alphabet has never been fully implemented in book form, the poet utilizes it on occasion, and always spells his own name as, "Klemente Soto Beles." The poems are also revolutionary in content: singing a hymn of praise to the international working class and its rebels, calling not only for the overthrow of those who hold political and economic power, but also for the demise of the words and ideas that cement oppression into place. He succeeds in placing the experience of the Puerto Rican laborer, and the quest for Puerto Rican independence, in a universal, even cosmic, context. Soto Vélez has written that the poet should act as: "blood/that/keeps/singing/after/it/congeals/to circulate/radiating through the insurrection/of its arteries."

Soto Vélez is, indeed, a poet of *La tierra prometida, The Promised Land.* That promised land is, of course, an independent Puerto Rico; the phrase also evokes the wanderings of the Puerto Rican diaspora, and the homeland it seeks; and, ultimately, the promised land, for Soto Vélez, represents an ideal workers' state wherever that may be found, with a corresponding fulfillment of human potential. The radical egalitarian vision of Soto Vélez is the driving force behind all his work, and thus the poems have the feel of impassioned prophecy, agitation in images of thunder and labor, lightning and blood, "subversive angels."

There are very few known published translations of poetry by Clemente Soto Vélez. None of his books have been published in translation. Though he has now, belatedly, been recognized as a national treasure in Puerto Rico, he is almost completely unknown in the United States beyond the Puerto Rican community, a casualty of the cultural blockade against Puerto Rican artists in this country. However, his words cannot be jailed like the man; for Puerto Ricans in particular, his words persist and inevitably endure. Soto Vélez himself pointed out this phenomenon when he wrote that he: "may as well have been born/wherever freedom/grows like children."

— Martín Espada and Camilo Pérez-Bustillo

The Blood
That Keeps Singing

*La sangre
que sigue cantando*

From

*Escalio
Fallow Land*

1937

Horizontes (fragmento)

—Las circunstancias—hablando entre nosotros—suelen lanzar, a veces, bromas un tanto pesadas. En realidad, el imperialismo es una broma de la ignorancia.

El imperialismo, en cualquier punto de la imaginación creadora, es la negación de la libertad.

Este libro—un libro no consiste en el número de sus páginas, sino en su elevación de lo justo y lo verdadero—, ha viajado a través de todos los torbellinos de la persecución. Ha estado en las manos íntimas de veraces revolucionarios; ha estado en los anaqueles de las imprentas; ha estado en la cárcel: siempre expuesto a ser absorbido por la ambición imperialista. Su autor,—mejor dicho, su compañero—, fue arrestado por el imperialismo, en el momento mismo en que escribía "La Revolución y lo Revolucionario", siéndole aplicado, además de la prisión, el destierro...

Horizons (excerpt)

—Circumstances—speaking among ourselves—sometimes tend to thrust cruel practical jokes upon us. In truth, imperialism is a joke made out of ignorance.

Imperialism, at any point in the creative imagination, is the denial of freedom.

This book—a book does not consist of the number of its pages, but rather the degree to which it upholds the just and the truthful—, has traveled through all the whirlwinds of persecution. It has been in the intimate hands of honest revolutionaries; it has been on the shelves of printers; it has been in jail: always subject to being absorbed by imperialist ambition. Its author—better said, its compañero—, was arrested by imperialism, at the same moment he was at work writing "Revolution and the Revolutionary," with imprisonment, as well as exile, imposed upon him...

Soledad

Volar, solo, volar
sobre los cielos
de la imaginación
más encendida,
y, así, solo, crear,
crear el vuelo
infinito de la vida.

Pensar, solo, pensar,
como piensan las fuerzas
de la creación reunidas,
y, así, solo, solo,
solo, auscultar
el principio causal
que en la luz vibra.

Cantar, solo, cantar,
como cantan los átomos
la voluntad activa,
y, así, solo, cantar
como lo informa
la conciencia real
de la energia.

¡Soledad, soledad!
—nimbo de la atracción
que todo lo equilibra
en la fuerza vital
que lo repele,—
¡Soledad, soledad,
corazón de la vida!

Solitude

To fly, alone, to fly
over the skies
of the most fiery
imagination,
and, so, alone, to create,
create the infinite
flight of life.

To think, alone, to think
as all the gathered forces
of creation think,
and, so, alone, alone,
alone, to listen searching
for the original reason
that vibrates in the light.

To sing, alone, to sing,
as the atoms sing
the will in action,
and, so, alone, to sing
as the actual awareness
of energy
tells it.

Solitude, solitude!
—Nimbus cloud of magnetic attraction
that balances all
within the living force
that repels it,—
Solitude, solitude,
heart of life!

From

Abrazo interno
Internal Embrace

1954

La emoción lograda

Nuevas fuerzas sociales se amarran la cintura
con horizontes de alegría, saltando sobre empalizadas
de amargura, para izar sobre las cúspides de la pesadumbre,
desplegada a los vientos anaranjados del razonamiento
—símbolo revolucionario de liberación humana—
la bandera de la paz como corazón del universo.

Por encima del corazón del universo, captando
la esperanza de la voluntad colectiva, iluminadora
intensidad de la fe popular,
despertando lo infinito con las canciones libertadoras
que incorporan a la fructífera cultura de su liberación,
con la creciente unidad del pensamiento,
la acción y la palabra.
Cada niño, cada mujer, cada hombre
es camino de estrellas palpitantes,
por donde ha de pasar, noble, digna, triunfante,
con calor vivificante, la verdad objetiva.

No es para los pusilánimes
el montar los caballos de la cólera bien cultivada
por el inflexible domador de los acontecimientos;
ni es para ellos el árbol frutecido de la teoría,
abonado por el cejijunto jardinero de la práctica;
ni es para ellos el observar el caminante
amanecer silencioso del espíritu
—fósforo con que la materia enciende la lámpara del espacio—;
ni es para ellos el zumo de los celajes cargados de perspectivas,
a punto de convertirse en frutas maduras de coraje;
ni es para ellos el abrir las bellotas de los atardeceres
abarrotados de esperanzas seductoras.

The Achieved Emotion

New social forces wrap their waists
with jubilant horizons, leaping over the palisades
of bitterness, to hoist the flag of peace, over grief's summit,
like the universal heart
— revolutionary symbol of human liberation —
unfurling to the orange winds of reason.

Beyond the heart of the universe, to grasp
the hope of collective will, the illuminating
intensity of the people's faith,
awakening the infinite with liberating songs,
enveloping the fertile culture of that liberation,
with the growing unity of thought,
action and word.
Each child, each woman, each man
is a path of throbbing stars,
where unbiased truth will walk,
with living heat, generous, dignified, triumphant.

It is not for the fearful
to mount the horses of fury groomed
by the stern trainer of daily events;
not for them the flowering tree of theory
fertilized by the worried gardener of practice;
not for them to witness the walking,
silent awakening of the spirit—
the match with which matter lights the lamp of space—
not for them the cloud-sap full of visions,
on the verge of becoming the ripened fruits of rage;
not for them to open the acorn of afternoons
bursting with seductive hopes.

No es dado a los pusilánimes descubrir el amor
que juega al esconder en las celosas cercanías de las fronteras,
amor que hoy se transforma en fraternal abrazo de pueblos
enamorados,
que por tantos años buscaban
lo que ardía en sus propias entrañas;
y que ahora ellos mismos, fertilizando rosas de comprensión,
encendidos por la luz interna de su desarrollo,
entienden que es la llama secreta de la economía universal
la llama que corre por los caminos reales del conocimiento,
montada en la ingobernable audacia de lo que se desarrolla.

No es dado a los pusilánimes
probar la miel agradable de lo nuevo,
ni pasearse por las cumbres de los llanos agitados de la palabra,
llena de creadoras acciones contrapuestas
en chocantes remolinos de movimientos contrarios,
abrazándose al cuello de armonías delirantes
y hostiles a la sombra caduca de lo falso.

No es dado a los pusilánimes agarrarse a los alambres
eléctricos del pensamiento para probar el valor enrojecido
de las ideas que se distancian para acercarse más
las unas a las otras, en las distancias mismas que les sirven
de punto de separación y de atracción irresistible
y de repulsión sugeridora de atracción renovada.

No es dado a los pusilánimes ser hoy y ser mañana
y ser al mismo tiempo
la línea vertical de la emoción lograda!

The fearful are forbidden to discover love
that plays at hiding in the jealous enclosure of borders,
love that transforms today into the human embrace of loving
                                        peoples,
who searched many years
                    for what burned within their bowels,
and these same ones now, fertilizing roses of knowledge,
illuminated by the internal light of their evolution,
understand that the secret flame of the universal economy
is the flame which races over the sure path of knowledge,
mounted on the rebellious audacity of whatever evolves.

The fearful are forbidden
                        to taste the satisfying honey of the new,
or to stroll over the heights of the word's agitated plains,
full of creative actions in confrontation,
clashing whirlpools of contrary motion,
hugging the neck of delirious harmonies
hostile to the decrepit shadows of the dishonest.

The fearful are forbidden to grasp
the electric wires of thought, to test the incandescent bravery
of ideas which separate to come closer,
across the distance that is also
the point of irresistible separation and attraction
and the seductive repulsion of attraction renewed.

It is forbidden to the fearful to be today and tomorrow
and to be at the same time
the upright line of the achieved emotion!

Estrellas de cinco puntas

Manos con manos que tengan
estrellas de cinco puntas:
estrellas de cinco puntas
con estrellas sin estrella.
Manos que despierten suelos
con voces de carreteras
empapadas en sudor
de curvas que comen piedras.
Manos que amarren el aire
que abre a la guerra sus piernas
para beberse la sangre
joven de toda la tierra.
Manos que no sepan nunca
que mataron a sabiendas
y que mataron matando
sin matar todas las guerras.
Manos que corten los grillos
de sembrados entre rejas,
con tijeras de palabras
en alfabetos de siembras.
Manos que escuchen el grito
que se saca la cosecha
encinta de los arados,
en las zanjas de la lengua.
Manos que quemen el cielo
de la boca que se cierra,
por temor a que le pongan
hierro de sombras mineras.
Manos que conquisten juntas
los secretos de las yerbas
que suben por los tejados
rubios de la primavera.
Manos que aprieten las frutas
coloradas de las cercas
que alimentan los caminos

Five Pointed Stars

Hands grasping hands that would hold
five-pointed stars:
five-pointed stars
with starless stars.
Hands that would awaken the ground
with the voices of roads
saturated in the sweat
of curves that swallow stones.
Hands that would tie the wind
which opens its legs to war
to drink the young blood
of all the earth.
Hands that would never know
that they killed knowingly
and that they killed killing
without killing all wars.
Hands that would cut the stalks
of ground sown
between wrought-iron fences,
with scissors of words
in alphabets of seed.
Hands that would hear the shout
which gathers the harvest
pregnant from the ploughs,
in the furrows of the tongue.
Hands that would ignite the sky
of the mouth closing
in fear of the iron
emerging from miners' shadows.
Hands that together would conquer
the secrets of the grasses
that climb over the blond rooftiles of spring.
Hands that would press the red fruit
of fences
which feed the red pathways

rojos de mis entretelas.
Manos que absorban racimos
de luceros en sus células
y sientan en cada poro
el alfiler de las venas.
Manos que ensarten agujas
de pulsaciones sangrientas
con los pulmones del viento
que se arrastra en las aceras.
Manos con manos que esculpan
con buriles de azoteas
las sombras de las estatuas
que anduvieron sin cadenas.
Manos que prendan la estufa
del aliento, sin prenderla,
con dedales de esperanza
y panales de soleras.
Manos que guien sin guiar
trenes con ruedas sin ruedas
por raíles de alabanza
con acero sin vergüenza.
Manos que quemen la cárcel
sin recuerdo que recuerda,
donde mi sombra templaba
cinco guitarras de hogueras.
Manos que viertan la sangre
en la redonda ponchera
de la estrella parpadeante
que sale por mis arterias.
Manos que escriban con sangre
palmo a palmo epifonemas
con paladares de acero
en amapolas despiertas.
Manos que toquen un piano
de relámpagos sin tregua,
con arcoíris de dedos
y pentagramas en vela.

of my embroidered heart.
Hands that would absorb clusters
of morning-stars in their cells
and would feel the pinprick of veins
in each pore.
Hands that would thread needles
of bloodied pulsations
with the lungs of the wind
crawling along sidewalks.
Hands with hands that would sculpt
with terrace-chisels
the shadows of the statues
that walked without chains.
Hands that would light the stove
of breath, without lighting it,
with thimbles of hope
and honeycombs of crossbeams.
Hands that would steer the trains without steering
on wheels without wheels
through rails of praise
and steel without shame.
Hands that would burn the jail
with amnesiac memory,
where my shadow tempered
five guitars in the bonfires.
Hands that would pour blood
in the round punchbowl
of the flickering star
which shoots through my arteries.
Hands that would write morals
in blood, inch by inch,
with steel palates
in the mouths of waking poppies.
Hands that would play a piano
of relentless lightning,
with a rainbow of fingers
and vigilant pentagrams.

Manos que abran en la sangre
yemas con dedos sin yemas,
para que la vida viva
sin vivir sin que se muera.

Hands that would open in the blood
fingertips with fingers without their tips,
so that life can live
without living without dying.

From

Arboles
Trees

1955

Esos árboles

Esos árboles
que no se llenan
los bolsillos de aguaceros,
que no sólo viven
de verdes pensamientos
amarillos,
sino que les sacan
puntas a las hojas
para adelantarse
al rumbo venidero de sus frutos.

Esos árboles
que aprenden
con la lluvia
a no mojarse los pies
aun cuando el agua
les suba
a la cintura.

Esos árboles
que vuelan
sobre la cima de su identidad
para eliminar
su distinción;
que dividen
la nada entre su todo
para encontrar el número
que trabaja a deshora.
Esos árboles
que desamarran
el cansancio...
Esos árboles
que enderezan
las cuatro esquinas del orgullo
que el hombre nuevo

Those Trees

Those trees
that do not fill
their pockets with rainstorms,
that not only live
by green thoughts
yellowing,
but also sharpen
their leaves into points
that herald
the harvest of their fruit.

Those trees
that learn
from the rain
not to wet their feet
even as the water rises
to their waists.

Those trees
that fly
over the peak of their identity
to eliminate
the differences between them;
that divide
nothingness among the whole
to find the number
which labors at all hours.
Those trees
that loosen
their exhaustion...
those trees
which straighten
the four corners of pride
that the new humanity

elabora
en colmenas de amor,
para elevar
la emoción humana
a un grado en que el lenguaje
es júbilo
entre los brazos adorados del llanto.

Esos árboles
que desentrañan
crepúsculos hartos de auroras
con actitudes diáfanas,
agudizando espuelas
para revivir
la muerte de la muerte;
que cantan
para despertar
a los que pierden el oído
a causa de no oír
la alegre canción del llanto.

Esos árboles
que lavan
con el corazón
la casa deshabitada del cariño,
donde el llanto
no tiene tiempo
ni de llorar su muerte;
donde la esperanza
no espera
para desatarse en llamas
por la doliente
vecindad del desaliento.

Esos árboles
que ven la pena
salir corriendo

builds
into beehives of love,
to raise
human emotion
to the point where language
becomes ecstasy
held in the worshipped arms of tears.

Those trees
that disembowel
twilights gorged with sunrises
of translucent attitudes,
sharpening spurs
to revive
the death of death;
that sing
to awaken
those who are deafened
for failure to hear
the jubilant song of tears.

Those trees
that wash
the abandoned house of affection
with their hearts,
where crying
has no time
to mourn even its own death;
where hope
does not hesitate
to unleash itself in flames
through the pained
proximity of despair.

Those trees
that see pain
run and leap

a gritar por las ventanas,
anudando
la voz de los vecinos
para que puedan bajar
a despedirse
de su propia despedida.

Esos árboles
que meditan
sobre los que malbaratan
el caudal de su talento
para asegurarse
de que el sol no los comprenda,
—los que gastan
pródigamente
la mañana de la doncella
que está con dolores—
los que pisotean
la niñez de los caminos,
los que lo saben todo
menos lo que no saben.

Esos árboles
que dan testimonio
de su desaparecimiento
en la ausente aparición
de su presencia,
que descubren
en el manantial de su sed,
el agua que acrecienta
la sed del manantial,
que se beben
el semblante
de la claridad
para unir horizontes
que llevan en la frente
la medida del cielo;

shouting through the windows,
knotting
the neighbors' voices
so that they would sink down
parting
with their own departure.

Those trees
that contemplate
the ones who squander
the bounty of their talent,
to assure
that the sun will not understand them
—those who would
foolishly waste
the morning of a virgin
in labor—
those who trample
the infancy of the roads,
those who know everything
except what they do not know.

Those trees
that bear witness
to their own disappearance
in the absent apparition
of their presence,
that discover
in the wellspring of their thirst
the water that feeds
the thirst of the well,
that drink
the face
of clarity
to blend horizons
bearing the measure of sky
on the forehead;

que apuntan
con índices grupales
su ascensión permanente
de pasos escarlatas.

Esos árboles
que ponen
en tensión musical
céfiros de entusiasmo,
que aprenden a besar
—con exenta plenitud de sombra—
a las rosas
que se desenvuelven
envueltas en harapos;
que recogen
la luz que desechan las calles
para alumbrar las casas
que no pueden abrir
sus propias puertas.
Esos árboles
que aprietan
las manos de ángeles descalzos
para sentir la tierra
gritar
entre sus dedos

....

Esos árboles
que saben libertarse
de la podredumbre del olvido,
de los amaneceres
que no saben amanecer
por detrás de su aurora,
del ensueño
que no sabe
poner a caminar su paradero,

that signal
with fused fingers
their eternal climb
of bright red steps.

Those trees
that set
sea-breezes of enthusiasm
into musical tension,
that learn to kiss
the roses
unfolding their rags
with the absolved abundance of shadows;
that collect
the light wasted by the streets
to illuminate the houses
that cannot open
their own doors.
Those trees
which shake
the hands of barefoot angels
to feel the earth
shout
between their fingers

....

Those trees
which know how to free themselves
from the putrefaction of forgetfulness,
from the daybreak
not knowing how to rise
behind its aurora,
from the dream
not knowing how to begin
the journey to its resting place,

del recuerdo
que no sabe sonsacar
el sembradío de sus pisadas,
para no tener que cortar
ganchos de pesadumbre.

Esos árboles
que saben pintar
la alborada de los huertos,
vaticinando
los senos levantados
de la próxima cosecha;
que enriquecen
la pobreza del silencio
para que los ojos que no duermen
se acerquen
a su sueño vertical;
que sorprenden
el sentimiento por sus pasos
en el momento en que el otoño,
—trabajador en oro—
comienza a deshojar la primavera.

Esos árboles
que anticipan su llegada
en el silencio de sus trinos,
para dejar a punto de salir
por la palabra
la aurora de su sangre,
que presienten
el dulce acíbar del acercamiento
que se aleja de la madrugada
aproximándose a la madrugada.

from memory
not knowing how to steal
the furrows of its footsteps,
not forced to cut
the hooks of grief.

Those trees
that know how to paint
the dawn of orchards,
foretelling
the raised breasts
of the next harvest;
that enrich
the poverty of silence
so that sleepless eyes
would come nearer
to their standing dream;
that surprise
emotion in its path
at the moment when autumn
—that goldsmith—
starts to strip the leaves of spring.

Those trees
which anticipate arrival
in the silence of birdsong,
to leave blood's daybreak
on the brink of emerging
through the word,
that sense
proximity's sweet harshness
drawing away from the depths of night
approaching half-light.

Esos árboles
que están ansiosos por ver
el alumbramiento feliz
de la niña
que desea vivamente
nacer iluminada
para desenterrar
la eternidad
que acaba de llegar
cuando sale su entierro.

Esos árboles
que en la florecida
tranforman la persona universal
en la canción que pasa
sobre su meridiano...

Those trees
that anxiously await
the celebrated birth
of the girl
who fiercely hopes
to be born enlightened
to exhume
eternity
that arrives at the moment
of its own burial.

Those trees
that in their flowering
metamorphosize the universal being
into the song passing
over its meridian...

From

Caballo de palo
The Wooden Horse

1959

#3

Lo conocí
viviendo
como una h encarcelada en la miel de sus abejas,
pero eran dulce amargo las rejas de la miel,
y por haberse enamorado
de la libertad
perdidamente,
y por no renunciar
a su amor ni ella a su amante,
la tierra para él
es huracán de estrellas perseguidas,
porque la libertad no puede ser
amante
sino de quien ama
a la tierra con su sol y su cielo.

#3

I came to know him,
living
like an h incarcerated in the honey of his bees,
but the bars of honey were bittersweet,
and because
he lost himself
in love with liberation,
and because he did not abandon
his love nor she her lover,
the earth for him
is a hurricane of persecuted stars,
since liberation cannot
love anyone
except whoever loves
the earth, with its sun and sky.

#4

Lo conocí
cojiendo
madrugadas de Lares despistado
por la majia morena de un requiebro de lunas
que corre
con un astro en los hombros,
remozado de ensueño,
como una mitolójica diosa de cucubanos.

Lo conocí
escuchando
indieras de tambores
montadas en recuerdos de caballos taínos
que atraen
las sicilianas en sus tardes de estiércol,
jugando alalimón con fuentes sin zapatos,
como alegres muchachas y muchachos
olorosos a frutas de noches deleitables.

Lo conocí
dejando
siestas de mariposas
para echarse
en la falda un racimo de cielo
que lleva
en el cuadril
un jirasol que canta
junto a la soledad carnal que se aúpa
en su estrella.

Lo conocí
velando
la bahía degollada por donde va
San Juan remando

#4

I came to know him
gathering
early mornings of Lares lost
in the brownskinned magic of quivering moons
that run
bearing a star on their shoulders,
rejuvenated in dreams,
like a mythic goddess of fireflies.

I came to know him
listening
to Indian ceremonies of drums
mounted on memories of Taíno horses
that lure
the Sicilian blossoms in their afternoons of manure,
playing a singsong game shoeless in the fountains,
like jubilant girls and boys
smelling of the fruit from delectable nights.

I came to know him
leaving
the siesta of butterflies
to toss
a handful of sky into the skirt
carrying
a sunflower that sings
in its folds
together with the solitude of the flesh hoisting itself
onto its star.

I came to know him
keeping vigil
over the beheaded bay
where San Juan goes rowing

sus amores, con Salomé en los ojos
de pueblos florecidos,
dando su testimonio de gracia anochecida
por el pavor de un beso acuchillado.

Lo conocí
ordeñando
cabras de retentiva histórica
como ondas rumiantes de mejillas taínas,
donde el atardecer de sus bocas rosadas
es una resonante jeneración de púrpura
que anda
ya por los astros con los pies en la tierra.

Lo conocí
soleando
el pensamiento en corrales de bruma
como una insurrección nueva de jirasoles,
tañedora de flautas de maíz
de entendimiento núbil,
que hace volar
la fe sobre marejada indócil de arcoíris.

Lo conocí
iniciando
piedras descamisadas en donde ya el estómago
no es
una frustración
hollando entre luciérnagas,
sino maizal que sube
la voz de sus espigas
hasta la resonancia
de un allá
empapado de pueblo.

Lo conocí
salvando soles osificados con la sangre purísima
que entona

his lovers, with Salome in the eyes
of flowering peoples,
giving testimony of grace at nightfall
in the terror of a mutilated kiss.

I came to know him
milking
goats of historical memory
like musing waves of Taíno cheekbones
where the dusk of their pale red mouths
is a resonant blooming of purple
still walking
among the stars with feet on the earth.

I came to know him
sunning
intelligence in corrals of fog,
like a new insurrection of sunflowers,
playing corn flutes
of nubile understanding,
giving flight
to faith over a restless sea-swell of rainbows.

I came to know him
initiating
shirtless stones where the stomach
is not now
frustration
trampling fireflies,
but rather a cornfield that raises
the voice of its growing stalks
far off as the echo
of a distant place
drenched in the people.

I came to know him
saving petrified suns with the purest blood
that intones

la palabra
donde la muerte corriente
no excita
como el diamante que canta
para oír la canción de sus huesos.

Lo conocí
representando
imajénes de fragancias incrédulas
para fecundar
el óvulo del acto de entender
con células de eternidad brevísima
como el espacio cósmico
en expansión perpetua.

Lo conocí
dando
asilo a las menesterosas madrugadas que llevan
en los lomos la luz
doliente del descuido:
frío oscuro que jira
lentamente acabándose
como un cuerpo sensible
que ansía
la extinción de su muerte.

Lo conocí
defendiendo
a las piedras que velan
su mañana con la resignación
cabal de sus fulgores
—meditativos espíritus pétreos,
verdades de barro,
costillas lucientes
que hacen
despuntar la expresión que transforma
su ser a cada paso.

the word
where commonplace death
fails to excite
like the diamond that sings
to hear the song of its bones.

I came to know him
reflecting
images of incredulous fragrances
to fertilize
the ovum in the act of understanding
with cells of the most fleeting eternity
like cosmic space
in perpetual expansion.

I came to know him
giving
asylum to the destitute dawns that carry
the sorrowful light of neglect
in their loins:
cold darkness that whirls
slowly stopping
like a feeling body
that longs
for the extinction of its death.

I came to know him
defending
his morning with the consummate resignation
of his brilliance
to the vigilant stones
—rocky contemplative spirits,
truths of mud,
luminous ribs
that cause
the sprouting of the expression that transforms
its being at each step.

Lo conocí
sumerjiendo
su caballo de palo en el agua negrísima,
donde la fantasía relumbra
como virtud que cae
alzándose
hasta su frente injenua,
donde la muerte arquea
la sombra de su espejo.

Lo conocí
juntando
oes acometedoras con aes reproductivas
cuando el cielo
es la i numeral que destella
en el sexo cursivo de la e primorosa
como una u alterada con piernas de diamante
donde aprende
la lengua a dar
a luz por su espíritu orgánico.

Lo conocí
saliendo
de la cáscara oscura que cae
del sol
dormida,
como una propaganda etérea de ojos claros,
desapesadumbrada,
flotante,
como la piel feliz
del efluvio fragante
de un presentimiento
que no se compadece
sino de su inclemencia.

Lo conocí
pereciendo
por el intacto vuelo:

I came to know him
submerging
his wooden horse in the blackest water,
where the imagination gleams
like integrity that falls
raising itself up
to its ingenuous forehead,
where death bends
the shadow of its mirror.

I came to know him
fusing
active ohs with reproductive ahs
when the sky
is the number i that flashes
in the sexual script of the elegant e
like an altered u with diamond legs
where the tongue
learns to give birth
through its organic spirit.

I came to know him
emerging
out of the dark husk that falls
from the sleeping
sun,
like an ethereal proclamation of clear eyes,
without grief's weight,
floating,
like the jubilant skin
of sweet-smelling exhalation
in foreboding
that does not pity itself
but rather its cruelty.

I came to know him
perishing
in his untouched flight:

latido soberano de elevación solícita,
piedra sensible con dureza de mar,
golpe que siente
el cristal eréctil de la forma,
corazón que golpea
su orijen en la sien.

Lo conocí
resistiendo
la obstinación amarilla del oro
—dúctil metal de terquedad de niebla—
que no deslumbra
a la atención que extiende
los brazos y estalla
como alba pertinaz
de azul acercamiento,
para que llegue
lo nuevo en lo acabado.

Lo conocí
tentando
la dureza paciente de ternuras calladas,
dolientes, como cielos doblados
que se echan
la tierra a la espalda
como inacabables seres que se yerguen
a enderezar los astros.

lordly pulsation of anxious heights,
a feeling stone with the hardness of the sea,
blow that feels
the erect crystal of form,
heart that strikes
its origin in the brow.

I came to know him
resisting
the yellow obstinance of gold
—malleable metal with the stubbornness of fog—
that does not dazzle
the attentiveness that stretches
its arms and bursts
like a determined dawn
of approaching blue,
so that the new
begins in what has ended.

I came to know him
touching
the patient hardness of silenced delicacy,
sorrowful, like folded skies
that throw
the earth onto the back
like the endless beings that stand straight
to set the heavens upright.

#14

Lo conocí,
rindiendo
homenaje de isla la aventura luciente
que, debajo del agua, pone
a prueba su muerte
ahogando lo inmortal, y el agua le devuelve
su experiencia mojada
como una flor que expira;
desaciertos como uñas de injuria desangran
la calma aborijen
a filo de pólvora y a humos de agravio,
pero aún la nostaljia resplandece
y jime en meditación que bebe
sus aguas,
pues su corazón
sigue como el indio recojiendo
estrellas.

#14

I came to know him,
offering
the island's homage in the shimmering dare
that, underwater, puts
the immortal's death by drowning
to the test, and the water washes up
his soaked knowledge
like an expiring flower;
blunders like claws of contempt drained blood
from the aboriginal quiet
at the sharp edge of gunpowder and the smoke of insult,
but still the longing gleams
and moans in the meditation that drinks
its waters,
so its heart
goes on like the Indian harvesting
stars.

#17

Y
siendo
así que aquellos que han burlado
el reino de la libertad
o su sustancia,
sufren
de excelsitud con ella sola,
sufren
de lucidez con ella sola,
no sufren
de soledad solos con ella,
sufren
de multitud solos con ella,
sufren
de placidez con ella sola,
sufren
de plenitud solos con ella,
sufren
de pequeñez con ella sola,
no sufren
de inmensidad solos con ella,
camaradas del amor,
amadla a ella,
camaradas de trabajo,
amadla a ella,
camaradas del mundo,
amadla a ella,
camaradas del cosmos,
ser de su estrella,
amadla a ella.

#17

And
since
those who have mocked
liberation's reign
or its essence
suffer
greatly with her alone,
suffer
in clarity with her alone,
and do not suffer
from solitude alone with her,
but suffer
in multitudes alone with her,
suffer
in tranquility with her alone,
suffer
in plenty alone with her,
suffer
in smallness with her alone,
but do not suffer
in immensity with her alone,
comrades of love
love her,
comrades of labor
love her,
comrades of the world
love her,
comrades of the cosmos,
be of her star,
love her.

#21

Clemente,
déjame llamarte
por tu nombre, aunque no sé
quién eres
ni intento
descubrirlo,
tus enemigos
guardan el retrato de tu nombre,
como la novia apasionada que porta
en su cartera la prenda del peligro,
para ir
de puerta en puerta
averiguando
si en el cielo no nacen
ángeles subversivos,
o si la tierra es
diosa que enamora
a los astros mientras están
dormidos,
o si la vecindad de tu cuerpo contiene
la predicción lumínica
de su ser cristalino,
o si es,
como la caída del sol,
aurora
en otro cuerpo.

Clemente,
por la sed que bebe
de tu estrella,
te digo
que yo moriré
antes que tú, porque muriendo
tengo que vivir

#21

Clemente,
let me call you
by your name, though I do not know
who you are
or intend
to find out,
your enemies
keep a portrait of your name,
like the passionate lover who carries
the amulet against danger in her purse,
going
from door to door
to ask if
subversive angels
are not born in the sky,
or if the earth
is a goddess that seduces
the stars while they
sleep,
or whether the closeness of your body holds
the luminous prophecy
of its crystalline being,
or whether it is,
like the sun's descent,
sunrise
in another body.

Clemente,
by the thirst that drinks
from your star,
I tell you
that I will die
before you, because in dying
I must live

por tu vida, sin que tú me conozcas
y sin yo conocerte,
pero es más importante saber
que no nos conocemos siendo
tan entrañables e íntimos amigos.

Muchos han muerto defendiendo
la espalda del hermano,
dulcemente,
esa dulzura ha de curar
mi terremoto de sospechas.

Mi amistad
es pura como el niño que acaba de nacer.

Yo sé
que el reino de tu amada
es más poderoso
que el reino estrellado de la muerte.

Yo sé
que la tierra no es
dichosa con los que nacen
para ser
arrastrados como yerbas pequeñas por los ríos,
los que la glorifican
trabajando,
glorifican la libertad en ella,
porque como tu edad
es tu amada
jugando entre las flores,
y en sus moradas deslumbrantes
es donde el hombre se gradúa
de hombre.

for your life, without you knowing me,
without me knowing you,
but more important understanding
that we do not know each other,
such deep and intimate friends.

Many have died defending
the back of a brother,
sweetly,
that sweetness must cure
my earthquake of suspicions.

My friendship
is pure as a child just born.

I know
that the dominion of your lover
is more powerful
than the starry kingdom of death.

I know
that the earth
takes no delight in those who are born
to be
dragged like short grasses by the rivers,
those who honor her
by working,
honor liberation within her,
since your age
is your lover
playing among the flowers,
and in their purple brilliance
humanity becomes
more human.

Y por eso tú no temes
a tu amada,
y por eso tú no temes
a los ojos de tu amada,
y por eso tú no temes
a los pasos de tu amada,
porque tu amada
es como río crecido creciendo
en la lengua de su amante.

Yo sé que tu tienes
muchísimos amigos,
pero yo nunca te dejaré
a deshora.

A la hora del relámpago,
muchas son
las flores que cuando azota
el huracán,
no dejan libar
a la abeja perseguida,
pero yo guardo
con la mía la espalda tuya,
y esto lo puedes escribir
con tu K de Clemente.

And that is why you do not fear
the one you love,
why you do not fear
your lover's eyes,
why you do not fear
you lover's footsteps,
because the one you love
is like a river arisen rising
on her lover's tongue.

I know you have
a multitude of friends,
but I will never leave you
in the wrong season.

At the hour of lightning,
when the hurricane thrashes,
there are many flowers
that do not allow
the persecuted bee
to sip,
but I will protect your back
with my own,
and this you can write
with your K for Clemente.

From

La tierra prometida
The Promised Land

1979

#2

la tierra prometida
es
canción solemne
de
asaltar
con desprendida nitidez el orijen
propagante
del cosmos
para que nuestro animal intelectivo
dirija
la insubordinación de la luz agredida
de la luz
que no
teme
deslumbrar
a su ser deslumbrante
a su ser anocheciente de luces delictivas
a su ser de canción consecuente
la tierra prometida
es
promesa
que brama
por el fuego
insubordinado del acto de entender
donde
la imponderabilidad de la palabra
es
cabalgar orijinal de oscuridad radiante
donde
es
el fuego fértil como alborear
frenético de una lengua feliz
donde
la ofensiva de la sensibilidad

#2

the promised land
is
a solemn song
attacking
the genesis
of the cosmos
with detached sharpness
so that our thinking animal
commands
the insubordination of victimized light
the light
that is not
afraid
of blinding
its dazzling being
its dusky being of delinquent lights
its being of honest song
the promised land
is
a promise
that roars
through the insubordinate fire
of understanding in action
where
the mystery of the word
is
the first gallop of radiant darkness
where
the fire is fertile
like the frantic dawning of a jubilant language
where
sensibility's offensive

es
asalto insistente de sensación asidua
o salud sibilante
saqueadora de ensueños
o irradiación de bruma
disolviéndose
donde
la intelijencia
es
bramido
asaltante
de clamor insurjente
alargándose
como una incursión de asíntotas mentales
por dentro de las ondas
que expande
la palabra
con que
recibe
la tierra prometida
a tu persona
poeta
o alba aguerrida
que se resiste
a pacificar
lo oscuramente claro
desde
donde
comienzan
ya
a apuntar
palomas de amaneceres subversivos
que degluten
el vuelo
de su orijen rámeo

is
the insistent attack of hardworking sensation
or hissing health
plunderer of illusions
or the glowing of fog
dissolving itself
where
intelligence
is
the attacking
roar
of insurgent clamor
lengthening
like the incursion of mental geometry
within the waves
that broaden
the word
with which
the promised land
receives
you
poet
or the war-wasted dawn
that resists
the pacification
of dark clarity
from
where
doves of subversive sunrises
now
begin
to take aim
to swallow
the flight
of their branching origin

para
hender
la hondura del indicio
no
es
paloma orijinal
la tierra prometida
que no
alarga
sus alas
hasta
distinguirse
de la totalidad de sus partes diversas
hasta no
ser
calma de alas tempestuosas
o acaballadero de yeguas enyescadas
por un olor
a luz
desenfrenada
que sólo
suele
asir
la brisa del deseo
donde
auroran
los brazos de sílabas salvajes
entre truenos pacíficos
de lengua guerrillera
donde la soledad
da
su virjinidad al héroe asesinado
para que nunca

to
crack
the fathoms of the sign
the promised land
is
not
the original dove
that does not
spread
its wings
until
it separates
from the sum of its diversity
not
becoming
the calm of its tempestous wings
or a stable of mares set ablaze
by the smell
of unleashed
light
that only
keeps
clutching
at the breeze of desire
where
the arms of savage syllables
are suns rising
in the peaceful thunderclaps
of the guerrilla tongue
where solitude
surrenders
its virginity to the murdered hero
so that heroism
never

muera
de sed la heroicidad
la heroicidad que nunca
es
proposición suicida
es mostrar
el misterio su flor reproducida
es
el héroe la flor
que
aroma
a la guerrilla de poesía guerrillera
con la sangre
que
desata
la palabra disidente
donde
arengan
los relámpagos
que renuncian a ser
mensajeros de plumas

dies
of thirst
that heroism which
is never
a suicidal gesture
is the mysterious revelation
of its multiplying blossom
the hero
is
the blossom
scenting
the guerilla band with guerilla poetry
with the blood
that
unchains
the dissident word
where
bolts of lightning
harangue
refusing to become
feathered messengers

#8

la tierra prometida
es
estrella gramínea
que no
implora
a los astros
es
cuervo
que no
frustra
la hora de su muerte expresiva

#8

the promised land
is
a grassy star
that does not
plead
with the heavens
is
a crow
that does not
elude
the hour of its eloquent death

#17

la tierra prometida
es
forma que
sufraga
esperanzas de prontitud caótica
o caos de acústica acosada
caos
deseable con oes de deseo
que abre
el esfínter secreto de la desobediencia
con la iluminación oscurísima
que un
verso
da
a otro verso
en la revolución de su ser
a su no ser lingüístico
para no
atollarse
en llanuras de palabras gallardas
no
es
forma que
ofrece
frenesí de empíreos
en desuso
defraudando
la acción
de
volar
no
es
metáfora de altura lampadófora

#17

the promised land
is
form that
cultivates
hopes of chaotic quickness
or chaos of persecuted acoustics
chaos
desirable with ohs of desire
that opens
the secret sphincter of disobedience
with the darkest illumination
that a
verse
gives
to another verse
in the revolution of its being
towards its linguistic nonbeing
so as not
to be mired
on the plain of elegant words
is
not
the form that
offers
a frenzy of utopias
in ruin
cheating
the action
of
flight
is
not
the metaphor of lamp-lit heights

que
ignora
su oscuridad de mano de marfil
no
es
esfera celeste
desnucando
la alegría musical de protestas
obreras
donde la belleza del calor colectivo
no
destierra
las piernas estelares del deleite
donde la rosa fragante del corazón
brilla
con magnitud
de obrero
creador
porque la rosa
no
es
bella
sino cuando las manos obreras
la
cultivan
porque la rosa
que
denigra
a las manos obreras
renuncia
a la intención de su perfume
porque el obrero
es
rosa del universo
o aroma de mano encantadora
porque la canción del obrero universal

that
ignores
the darkness of its ivory hand
is
not
the celestial sphere
garroting
the musical exhilaration
of laborers' protests
where the beauty of collective heat
does not
exile
the stellar legs of delight
where the sweet-smelling rose of the heart
gleams
with the greatness
of the worker-creator
because the rose
is
not
fine
unless the workers' hands
cultivate
it
because the rose
that
disgraces
the workers' hands
abandons
the purpose of its perfume
because the worker
is
the rose of the universe
or aroma of the conjuring hand
because the song of the universal worker

es
resistencia embellecedora
contra la esperanza torturante
del parásito social
que
prefiere
morir
como espejo carnívoro
antes que
ser
testigo ocular de su entierro
donde la eternidad
se
quita
su vestido
para
enardecer
su excelencia
con halagos de muerte amotinada
o primor preposicional
de pradera
a prueba de propósito
obrero de la factoría del intelecto
obrero de garganta de argamasa
fábrica fabulosa de asaltos con alas
selectivas
cuando a tu sien
la
escinde
el ogro del orgullo agresor
la eternidad
es
ternura brillantísima
de la insubordinación segura de su sangre
a quien
canta
la muerte malherida

is
resistance that brings grace tò bear
against the tormenting hope
of the social parasite
who
prefers
to die
like the carnivorous mirror
before
becoming
the eyewitness to his own burial
where eternity
strips
to
inflame
its excellence
with flattery of mutinous death
or prepositional dexterity
of the pasture
that is purpose-proof
worker of intellect's factory
worker of the cemented throat
fabled factory of attack with selective
wings
when
the ogre of the invader's pride
cuts
into your forehead
eternity
is
the incandescent tenderness
of its blood's sure insubordination
to which
mortally wounded death
sings

de la muerte vital de la esperanza
la esperanza
que
es
desesperación serenísima
del trabajador obrero
o del obrero trabajador
que
industrializa
la gloria de la fábrica
entre alabanzas con brazos de carbón
para que la sensación
desenfrene
su acémila
de militancia límpida
como la guerrillera
que
delega
en otra guerrillera
el porvenir de la lucha a muerte
cuando la sangre del valor
se
lava
con su sangre
como el nunca lisiado sonido
de una sílaba
que se
interpone
en el entendimiento
como espina dorsal de los muertos
que
cantan
para que los guerrilleros de la palabra
asesinada
canten

of hope's vibrant death
the hope
that
is
the most serene desperation
of the laborer-worker
or the worker-laborer
who
industriously creates
the holiness of the factory
amid praises waving with arms of coal
so that feeling
unbridles
its mule
of clear militancy
like the woman guerrilla
who
entrusts
to another
the future of the struggle till death
when the blood of courage
washes
itself
with its blood
like the never-wounded sound
of a syllable
that
intrudes
into understanding
like the backbones of the dead
that
sing
so that the guerrillas of the murdered
word
could sing

tanto en el lenguaje clandestino
como en la clandestinidad del lenguaje
porque no
es
metabólico el amanecer
de los perseguidores del espíritu
porque no
es
constructora la palabra
que no
es palabra destructora
porque
es la vida la lengua de la muerte
sin otra escapatoria
que
vencer
a las dos
para
ser
arquitecto de cráter universal
donde
es
dios estudiante
de asignaturas líricas
como un churumbel de chozas desechadas
donde pedúnculos podadores de piedra
son
ya
impedimento desatado
o trabajador
que
articula
su curso de matrícula atroz
para
desagradar
a la gratitud

as much in clandestine language
as in the clandestinity of language
because
the dawn
of those who persecute the spirit
is
not metabolic
because the word
is
not a builder
without being
a destroyer
because
life is the tongue of death
with no other escape
but
to conquer
both
to
be
architect of the universal crater
where
god is a student
of lyrical assignments
like an oboe of despised shacks
where stalk-pruners of stone
are
still
the unleashed obstacle
or laborer
who
articulates
the course of horrible matriculation
to
displease gratitude

la gratitud
que
es
gracia desagradante
donde la agresión
se
gradúa
entre gritos groseros
para
desintegrar
lo agradecido
para
desintegrar
los gerundios en jermen
del nuevo lenguaje social del obrero
a quien
insiste
en
embrutecer
el seductor acaudalado
con la sangre primorosa del obrero explotado
hasta su enunciación
funeral
trabajador
tu
eres
ensueño mañanero
diciendo
tus auroras
a la tierra
que
arriesga su amor a cambio de tu desventura
para que te
rebeles
contra los detractores de su preñez señera
su forma

the gratitude
that
is
irritating grace
where aggression
climbs
through obscene shouts
to
disintegrate
things gratefully received
to
disintegrate
seedling gerunds
of the new social language of the worker
willfully
kept
ignorant
by
the wealthy deceiver
with the exquisite blood of the exploited worker
until
the eulogy
worker
you
are
the sun rising in dreams
speaking
your auroras
to the earth
that
risks its love in exchange for your misery
so that you
rebel
against the slanderers of your solitary pregnancy
its form

revelando
la producción de tus brazos artísticos
trabajador
en tus manos
la eternidad
reside
en esa residencia
vive
la libertad

revealing
the labor of your artisan's arms
worker
eternity
lives
in your hands
in those hands
lives
liberation

#18

la tierra prometida
eres
tú
desde ti
truena
la intuición esquiva
o fiera
que
anhela
humanizarse
en sistema social de precisión celeste
donde tú
eres
ira de jirasol
que
jira
hasta contra la revolución solar
o vuelo de la luz aritmética
para
entender
que
eres tú
sonoridad de persona viva
entre sonidos de contiendas inhóspitas
porque desde ti
la función
de enjendrar
se
propaga
como síntoma de motines
armónicos
donde
orijinan
cosmonautas mentales

#18

You
are
the promised land
from you
thunders
the elusive or fearsome
intuition
that
craves
the human in itself
in a social system of celestial precision
where you
are
the fury of the sunflower
that whirls
even against the sun's revolution
or the flight of mathematical light
so as to
understand
that
you are
the resonance of a living being
amid the dissonance of struggle
because out of you
fertility
gives birth to itself
like an omen
of harmonious uprisings
where
cosmonauts of the mind
create

auroras
contendientes
para
sorprender
asilos de asaltos
seductores
la tierra prometida
no
es
indicación con brazos de mal venidero
no
es
efluvio confortante de inflicción agorera
donde
estuprar
moradas no
es
ya costumbre lírica
donde
las madrugadas enérgicas del ánimo
brillan
como pechos obreros
o umbrales palabróforos
por donde el universo
entra
como abanderado de la imajen poética
o forma de la luz
desatada

warlike
dawns
to
ambush
the sanctuaries of seductive
attack
the promised land
is
not
a sign with arms of approaching danger
is
not
the comforting flow of prophetic injury
where
the plundering
of mansions
is
not
yet a lyrical tradition
where
the brillant early mornings of the spirit
gleam
like the chest of a laborer
or word-forged thresholds
where the universe
enters
like the torchbearer of the poetic image
or the form of light
unleashed

#29

poeta
tu
eres
humanización de la luz
por el materializado amor
del deseo
de
ser
asaltador de la inmortalidad
de
ser
transduración efímera
como fuente perenne
que arguye
en contra de su forma
o
sangre
que
sigue
cantando
después
de
conjelarse
para
circular
radiantemente por la insurrección
de sus arterias
poeta
la inmortalidad
es
ensambladura de aledaños
bisoños
no habituados
a la acción de delinquir

#29

poet
you
are
light transformed into humanity
through the tangible love
of desire
to
be
the attacker of immortality
to
be
transcendent enduring ephemeral
like a perpetual fountain
that bends arguing
against its own form
or
blood
that
keeps
singing
after
it
congeals
to
circulate
radiating through the insurrection
of its arteries
poet
immortality
is
the architecture of borders
wild
unaccustomed
to subversive action

como la comodidad del pensar pervertido
humanización de la luz
eres
tú
poeta
o pecho alado del entender egrejio
desde donde todos
los hombres
o
todas las mujeres
dan
sustancia a su esencia

like the comfort of corrupted thought
poet
you
are
light into humanity
or breast with wings of profound understanding
from where all
men
or
all women
give
substance to their existence

#35

la tierra prometida
se
identifica
con las manos del peón desatendido
por el paladar
de la opulencia
con las manos
del peón
que
narran
la miseria social
que
rubrica
su cara profética
con las manos
del peón
que
compran
la alegría
empinando
el codo del amanecer
para dar
molde melódico
a la sensibilidad de su excelencia
con las manos
del peón
que
manejan
haciendas de cuchillos
para moldear
su aurora
con las manos
del peón

#35

the promised land
becomes
one
with the hands of the shunned peon
through the palate
of opulence
with the hands
of the peon
that
tell of
social misery
which
marks
his prophetic face in red
with the hands
of the peon
that
trade
in the joy
bending
the elbow of drunken daybreak
to give
melodic cast
to the sensibility of his excellence
with the hands
of the peon
that
manage
haciendas of knives
to mold
his aurora
with the hands
of the peon

que
truenan en los cartílagos del porvenir
con las manos
del peón
que
reprenden
a los orfebres de la depredación
para que no
se hurte
el sabor del saber
con las manos
del peón
que
dependen
del día de sus brazos
para
elevarse
en la mañana de sus piernas
sobre su sangre desbordada
con las manos
del peón
que
dependen
del día de sus brazos
para
elevarse
en la mañana de sus piernas
sobre su sangre desbordada
con las manos
del peón
que
son
rocío de poesía inusitada
con frescor de frenesí
perfecto
como violenta perturbación del ánima
que
abre

that
thunder in the cartilage of the future
with the hands
of the peon
that
push away
the goldsmiths of plunder
so that
the savored taste of knowledge
is not stolen
with the hands
of the peon
that
depend
on the day of his arms
to
rise
on the morning of his legs
over his brimming blood
with the hands
of the peon
that
depend
on the day of his arms
to
rise
on the morning of his legs
over his brimming blood
with the hands
of the peon
that
are
rainshowers of uncommon poetry
with a fresh breeze of frenzy
perfect
like the violent confusion of spirit
that
opens

de par en par sus puertas
a los amaneceres
más insubordinados
con las manos
del peón
que
arrebatan
a lo porvenir
el porvenir
que
brama
persiguiendo
su brújula
con las manos
del peón
que
rechazan
henchir
sus pechos
de anchura anochecida
con las manos del peón
que
siembran
sentimientos de sol
para
ser
ruiseñor
que no
duerme
cantando
a su existencia
con las manos
del peón
que
matriculan
el universo

its doors wide
to the most
insubordinate sunrises
with the hands
of the peon
that
snatch
the future away
from what it would become
the future
that storms
following
its compass
with the hands
of the peon
that
reject
inhaling
dusky latitudes
with the hands of the peon
that
plant
sensations of sun
to
become
the nightingale
that does not
sleep
singing
to his existence
with the hands
of the peon
that
enlist
the universe

para que
aprenda
a
cantar
como el peón del verbo subversivo
con las manos del peón
que
condecoran
su cuerpo maltratado
con tallos de estallidos
o truenos
desensillados
con las manos del peón
que
devoran
la bruma prejuiciada
de la posesión insensible
que
aúlla
como olfato de bestia malherida
con las manos del peón
que aun
se
reciben
de doctoras
en la universidad de la hoz
o del martillo
con las manos del peón
que
abogan
por
ciudadanizar
las ubres enamoradas
de la canción
de lo desconocido
con las manos del peón
que
agremian

so that it would
learn
to
sing
like the peon of the subversive verb
with the hands
of the peon
that
dignify
his abused body
with sprouts of gunfire
or unsaddled
thunderclaps
with the hands
of the peon
that
swallow
the biased haze
of callous possession
that
howl
the sniffing of a badly wounded beast
with the hands of the peon
that still
receive
their doctorates
at the university of the sickle
or the hammer
with the hands of the peon
that
advocate
naturalization
for udders enamored
of the song
for the unknown
with the hands of the peon
that
unionize

jerundios de verbos ajitados
con las manos del peón
que no
enjaulan
agitaciones jóvenes
aun cuando
se les
ordene
o si no
serán
tiroteadas
o asesinadas
con las manos del peón
que domestican
neblinas bicéfalas
con las manos del peón pensador
que
son
las espaldas de la palabra
peón de la palabra
que la palabra
sea
tu peona

gerunds of flurrying verbs
with the hands of the peon
that do not
cage
youthful agitation
even when
so
ordered
or else
to be
sprayed with bullets
murdered
with the hands of the peon
that tame
the two-headed clouds
with the hands of the thinking peon
that
are
the backbones of the word
peon of the word
let the word
become
your servant

#65

la tierra prometida
es
quimificación
donde el entendimiento
embalsama
su cadáver
para el laboratorio
del deseo
disidente
para
normalizar
el alma enamorada de la luz
que
no
alcanza
a
verse
sucumbida
porque
es
fermentadora la forma de la muerte
ser
lares
es
no
ser
deblegación de cerviz clausurada
ser
lares
es
ser
duración indómita
empedrada de potros de piedra
que
doma

#65

the promised land
is
the alchemy
where understanding
embalms
its cadaver
for the laboratory
of dissident
desire
to
normalize
the enamored soul of light
that
does not
allow
itself
to be
dominated
because
the shape of death is a fermenting agent
to be
Lares
is
not
to be
the bowing of the cloistered neck
to be
Lares
is
to be
indomitable durability
cobbled with foals of stone
that
tames

la niñez
del entendimiento
con precisión de sicilianas
que
ponen
a
pensar
la luz de su destierro
ser
lares
es
no
ser
conuco de tabonuco eunuco
ser
lares
es
ser
cabal acabamiento
de labios de escabel
ser
lares
es
ser
ovación de alcobas
con clavículas cálidas
ser
lares
es
ser
jardín
que
jura
por su perfume
purificar
su aroma
ser
lares

the childhood
of understanding
with the precision of Sicilian blossoms
who
begin
to
think
through the light of their exile
to be
Lares
is
not
to be
the field of the castrated tree
to be
Lares
is
to be
the consummate end
of the stool's lips
to be
Lares
is
to be
the ovation of bedrooms
with warm collarbones
to be
Lares
is
to be
a garden
that
swears
by its perfume
to purify
its aroma
to be
Lares

es
ser
furia aurífera
que
no
trafica
con infartos de anáforas
no
ser
lares
es
ser
enclaustramiento bloqueador de claveles
ser
lares
es
ser
clima reclutador
de clamor clandestino

is
to be
gold-bearing fury
that
does not
traffic
in heart attacks of rhetorical repetition
not
to be
Lares
is
to be
the smothering blockade of carnations
to be
Lares
is
to be
the inciting climate
of clandestine clamor

AFTERWORD: UN EJERCITO DE IDEAS

Palabras de introducción por Clemente Soto Vélez al Primer Conclave Cultural Latinoamericano en Massachusetts, Centro Cultural Jorge N. Hernández, Villa Victoria, Boston, 25 de septiembre, 1987 (fragmento)

Compañeros y Compañeras:

...Aquí en Boston, tenemos compañeros y compañeras de todas las nacionalidades, y como formamos parte de esta colectividad fraternal, tenemos que entender que la fraternidad es la fuente que nos va a dar el poder para transformar la sociedad americana o norteamericana o latinoamericana en Boston. En razón de aquel, todos nosotros estamos sufriendo discriminación de una forma o otra. Y ese trabajo está en manos de ustedes. No me incluyo, porque no vivo en Boston, pero con el pensamiento trabajo con ustedes, desde Puerto Rico, desde Nueva York, dondequiera que esté, porque esta humanidad forma parte de mi persona, y mi persona se debe a ella. Cuando yo veo, por ejemplo, en Chile que la policia le raja la cabeza de un hermano nuestro, yo sufro. Yo sufro; me duele en el alma. O en Nueva York, o en California, o en Nicaragua, o en El Salvador, o dondequiera que sea. A mí me duele porque la humanidad no es más que una. No son dos. Y yo formo parte de esa humanidad. [Yo siento] el dolor que produce un macetazo dado en la forma, con la ira que lo hacen los que cargan las armas en la mano, esos mismos que comen y viven del trabajo de todos los hermanos a quienes ellos golpean. Y por eso digo yo que hay que ver todo lo que es este esfuerzo personal de ustedes, sencillamente como hermanos.

Somos latinoamericanos, sí, es verdad, y tenemos que luchar por los intereses latinoamericanos, y tratar de juntarlos a todos de manera tal que formamos una especie de ejército: un ejército de ideas para transformar a aquellos que no progresan, y tienen que progresar. Entendemos que así está compuesta la humanidad también: de elementos que progresan y otros que no progresan.

AFTERWORD: AN ARMY OF IDEAS

Opening remarks by Clemente Soto Vélez to the Conclave Cultural: the First Latino Arts and Humanities Conference in Massachusetts, held at the Jorge N. Hernández Cultural Center, Villa Victoria, Boston, on September 25, 1987 (excerpt)

Compañeros and Compañeras:

...Here in Boston, we have compañeros and compañeras of all nationalities, and since we are all part of this familial collectivity, we must understand that this sense of brotherhood is the source that will give us the power to transform American or North American or Latin American society in Boston. Because of that potential, all of us are subjected to discrimination in one form or another. And that work is in your hands. I don't include myself, because I don't live in Boston, but with my thoughts I labor with you, from Puerto Rico, from New York, from wherever I may be, because this humanity is part of my person, and my personhood flows from it. When I see, for example, that the police in Chile have split open the head of one of our brothers, I suffer. I suffer; it hurts me in the soul. Be it in New York, or in California, or in Nicaragua, or in El Salvador, or wherever it may be. This hurts me because there is only one humanity. There are not two. And I am part of that humanity. I feel the pain from a beating inflicted like that, with the rage of those who inflict it and load the weapons in their hands, those who eat and live from the labor of all the brothers and sisters they beat. That's why I say that all of your labors must be recognized, simply as brothers and sisters.

We are Latin Americans, yes, it's true, and we have to struggle in defense of Latin American interests, trying to bring all of us together in such a way that we form a kind of army: an army of ideas to transform those who do not progress, and must progress. We also understand that this is what all of humanity is composed of: elements that progress and those that don't

Pero la naturaleza misma nos dice a nosotros que eso es así. La naturaleza nos pone al lado de un volcán que se lleva por delante a una población entera en segundos y juntos, a un jardín de rosas lindísimas.

...Y es haciendo como se prueba que somos seres humanos capacitados dentro de nosotros mismos. Nosotros progresamos porque sencillamente nos obliga la naturaleza a progresar, y si no, nos morimos. Nos morimos en el sentido físico, y de seguro material, como se mueren las ideas. Toda idea que no es progresista o que es retardataria muere inmediatamente. No tiene validez. Pero la que no es retardataria, esa persiste, persevera. Corre, vuela, se convierte en aeroplano, se convierte en estrella, dependiendo de todos aquellos que la impulsen.

...Pero los retardatarios mentales no entienden que es tan sencillo. Y de allí nos encontramos tipos como, por ejemplo, este que gobierna a los Estados Unidos, o en Chile, o en cualquier parte del mundo, los reaccionarios que no creen esto. Es imposible hacerles entender estas cosas. El cambio está constantemente sucediendo dentro de ellos, pero no quieren aceptarlo. Ellos no lo entienden. La ambición del enriquecimiento material no les deja ver nada. Y de allí, cuando nosotros podemos transformar ese enriquecimiento, también, en enriquecimiento intelectual...o filosófico o artístico, en todos los ordenes, pues, nosotros los vencemos. Y se vence al enemigo. Al enemigo se vence sencillamente con la fuerza de las ideas, y me refiero al enemigo de la ignorancia, no a los ejércitos regidos por hombres.

...Yo les felicito a todos ustedes en mi nombre personal por lo poco que yo he podido aportar a la humanidad. Es muy poco, pero llevo ochenta y pico de años trabajando en esa misma dirección, y más nunca la dejaré sola a ella, porque ella son ustedes. Y como dice Soto Beles en *Caballo de palo*, a terminar:

progress. Nature itself tells us that this is so. Nature puts a volcano that can sweep away an entire city in seconds side by side with a garden of the most beautiful roses.

...And it is by doing this that we show that we are human beings capable of progressing. Progress is simply that which we carry inside ourselves. We progress simply because nature compels us to, and if not, we die. We die in a physical sense, and of course a material sense, as ideas die. Every idea that is not progressive or is backward dies immediately. It has no validity. But an idea that is not backward persists and perseveres. It runs, flies, becomes an airplane, becomes a star, depending on whoever gives it force.

...But those who are mentally backward do not understand how simple it is. And so we find characters like, for example, the one who governs the United States, or in Chile, or in any part of the world, reactionaries who do not believe this. It's impossible to make them understand these things. Change is constantly happening within them, but they don't want to accept it. They don't understand it. Their greed for material wealth does not allow them to see anything else. And that's why, when we can transform that wealth, too, into intellectual...or philosophical or artistic wealth, in all areas, well, then we triumph over them. And we overcome the enemy. We overcome the enemy, simply with the force of our ideas, and I refer to ignorance as our enemy, not to armies governed by men.

...I congratulate all of you in my own name, and that of the little I have been able to contribute to humanity. It's really very little, but I have been working for eighty-some years in the same direction, and I will never abandon [humanity], for she is all of you. And, as Soto Beles says, in *The Wooden Horse,* in closing:

A la hora del relámpago,
muchas son
las flores que cuando azota
el huracán,
no dejan libar
a la abeja perseguida,
pero yo guardo
con la mía la espalda tuya,
y esto lo puedes escribir
con tu K de Clemente.

Y con la K de todos ustedes, que representan estos intereses
universales.

At the hour of lightning,
when the hurricane thrashes,
there are many flowers
that do not allow
the persecuted bee
to sip,
but I will protect your back
with my own,
and this you can write
with your K for Clemente.

And with the K for all of you, who represent these universal
concerns.

Notes on the Translators

Puerto Rican poet and translator Martín Espada was born in Brooklyn, New York in 1957. He is author of three poetry collections: *The Immigrant Iceboy's Bolero* (Waterfront Press), *Trumpets From the Islands of Their Eviction* (Bilingual Press, Arizona State University), and *Rebellion is the Circle of a Lover's Hands*, also from Curbstone Press in a bilingual edition. For his poetry, he has been awarded a Massachusetts Artists Fellowship, a National Endowment for the Arts Fellowship, and the PEN/Revson Fellowship as well as the Paterson Poetry Prize for *Rebellion is the Circle of a Lover's Hands*. His translations have appeared in *Agni Review, Hanging Loose,* and the *Minnesota Review,* among other publications, and he was the founder of the Artists Foundation Translation Project, which matched Massachusetts writers working in Spanish or Chinese with translators nationwide, and funded the translation of their work. Espada currently lives in Boston, working as a tenant lawyer and supervisor of Su Clínica, a legal services clinical program for low-income tenants administered by Suffolk University Law School.

Translator, essayist, and civil rights lawyer, Camilo Pérez-Bustillo was born in Queens, New York, of Colombian parentage, in 1955. His work has appeared in the *Agni Review, Hanging Loose, Hispanic, Left Curve, Minnesota Review* and *Unity,* as well as *Nuevo Amanecer* in Nicaragua and *Tres Mil* in El Salvador. His translation of essays by Juan Antonio Corretjer, entitled *Poetry and Revolution,* is forthcoming in the Curbstone Press Art on the Line series, and he is co-translator, with Martín Espada, of Espada's *Rebellion is the Circle of a Lover's Hands.* Pérez-Bustillo currently lives in San Francisco, where he works with Multicultural Education, Training and Advocacy (META), Inc., a non-profit legal advocacy organization specializing in the educational and civil rights of immigrants and linguistic minorities. He is the President of the U.S. branch of the Asociación Americana de Juristas (American Association of Jurists), an anti-imperialist lawyers' association of the Americas. Pérez-Bustillo received a W. K. Kellogg National Foundation Fellowship in 1991.